JOURNEY
COMPANIONS

JOURNEY COMPANIONS
Poetry and Reflections
for Contemplation

Justin Simpson

POETRY CHAPEL
PRESS

Copyright© Justin Simpson 2022.

All rights reserved. No part of this publication may be reproduced, distributed, or transmitted in any form or by any means, without prior written permission of the respective author.

Poetry Chapel ® Press
Brisbane, QLD, Australia

Cover Illustration: by David Tensen

Also available in eBook.

Journey Companions / Justin Simpson.
ISBN 978-0-6456858-0-0

For Deb.

I love sharing the journey with you.

Contents

Endorsements

Introduction

1. Here We Are
2. Commune
3. Solitude
4. Fully
5. Journey Outwards
6. Connected
7. Foraging

Reflection: Way

8. Momentary Pause
9. Unitive
10. Contemplative
11. Fields
12. Deeply Shaped
13. Unseen
14. Worship

Reflection: Movement

15. Just the One
16. Greening
17. Inside Love
18. Pneuma
19. No Separation
20. Quietly Growing
21. Skimming Stones

Reflection: Sojourners

22. Awakening
23. Very Being
24. Heartbeat
25. Confluence
26. Lovingkindness
27. Animated
28. In the River

Reflection: Rest

29. The Cliffs
30. Participation
31. It's Being

Reflection: Perspective

Further Steps

Acknowledgements

Endorsements

Justin is an integral part of our Quaker meeting. As we have journeyed alongside him in his creation of this book, we have experienced the affective power of his poetry as a pathway to contemplation, creativity and community. This little book contains multitudes more than its small size suggests, inviting the reader into a deeper connection with one's self and others, and a quiet abiding in "everything that is God."

Friends Online Recognised Meeting, NSW Regional Meeting

I'm happy to commend Journey Companions, which invites the reader into a contemplative space. I think the poems and accompanying reflections could deeply encourage and enrich any reader's prayer life. I'm looking forward to using them.

Bruce Henry, Presiding Clerk, Quakers Australia

In a time in my own life when there is much going on – a baby, teenagers, and plenty of other pressures - these poems have been an unexpected gift for my soul. My own burdened praying is met here by the quiet patience of God, already around me. I breathe. Through short, accessible and profound words, with plenty of space on the page, a window is opened. I warmly commend not just this poetry, but the encounter to which Justin leads us, through it.

David Fotheringham, Moderator, Uniting Church Synod of Victoria and Tasmania

A leader leads from their convictions and Justin does so whole-heartedly. Exploring unfamiliar practices and being open to new insights has required his courage, intent and vulnerability. I have seen the journey profoundly shape Jus's discipleship, leadership and relationships. I am grateful for the modelling and invitation he shares in *Journey Companions*.

Naomi Swindon, Scripture Union Australia

Over the last six months I have been reading Justin's poems. When times have been a little hard, I have turned to Justin's poems and found great comfort in them. They guide me, gently, through the maze of uncertainty that surrounds us today.

Bryan Milne, Quaker friend

Justin's light-filled poems guided and encouraged me to be still and quietly reflect. To my surprise, this allowed the poetry of my own soul to blossom.

Maggi Storr, Quaker friend

In his poems, Justin shares his deepest thoughts, expresses his joy, and includes us in his contemplation quest. We have quickly grown to love the poet and his poetry. These poems are short, connect with the moment, then guide you to a special contemplative space.

Myrtle and Alan Trubody, Quaker friends

Journey Companions

Introduction

A few years back, David, a mentor and spiritual guide, encouraged me to try Centering Prayer and kindly challenged me to sit in stillness for twenty minutes twice a day. 'Impossible!', I thought. The experience often seems to involve eighteen minutes of noisy monkey mind, one minute of transition, and then one minute of golden silence. As a contemplative method, Centering Prayer involves using a simple word or phrase to let go of arising thoughts and return to being open to God in the present moment.

Somehow, over time, this prayer method has been slowly melting my incessant thought patterns and softening my ego-centred identity and worldview. Maybe this is because the practice allows more space, helping me to not cling to every thought. One way or another, it has profoundly reshaped my life and spiritual journey.

Contemplation and poetry have, for me, gone hand-in-hand. I started writing as a way of reflecting on what I was discovering with contemplative life. And like a friendship, the poems grew with layers of connection and meaning.

The suggestion for this book came from a friend named Myrtle, a vibrant lady in her eighties, a Quaker elder and gifted artist. She said she could see my poems as a book which someone could carry around and draw on each day.

So one way you can engage with this book is as a daily companion. Read a poem each day and let it influence you along with contemplation, meditation, journaling or other spiritual praxis. At the end of each week and month, explore the guided reflection and practice, considering an aspect of your journey - the way of love, movement, travelling companions, rest and perspective. Alternatively, you may want to read right through the book and allow the poems to connect with you in different ways. You could read them with another person or group of friends, participating in the contemplative journey together.

You may notice there is considerable white space in this book. This is to give you room for your own journaling, questions, responses and creative expression. In whatever ways you engage with these poems and reflections, I hope they become companions for your own journey with contemplation, creativity and community.

Justin

Wurundjeri land, Melbourne, Australia

Justin Simpson

Journey Companions

1. Here We Are

Here
together in our meeting place
in this sacred space

Now
together for our appointment
this special moment

In love and purpose
mystery and wonder
here we are

2. Commune

Light
she comes to us

Stillness
he welcomes us

Being
they embrace us

and
we commune
together

3. Solitude

Perceiving stillness
   motionless trees
   a smooth lake
   my quieting mind.

Sensing subtle movements
   those echoes
   the vibration in my hands
   our expanding love.

I experience your presence
in solitude.

With silence
I hear your voice.

4. Fully

The time is fulfilled.
It's right now
this moment.

The kingdom of God is at hand.
The Divine realm is among us
immediately accessible.

Change your ways.
Now live fully
in this realm.

Mark 1:15

5. Journey Outwards

An exploding star
thrusting stardust
in all directions

ancient gumtrees
releasing countless seeds
on the wind

the labyrinth path
winding from the centre
into new space

6. Connected

Look at the birds of the air.
All beings are deeply integrated
none are separated.

Walk in the fields. Look at the flowers.
Everything is profoundly connected
nothing's unrelated.

Can we add even an hour?
Reality now fully united
time is not added or divided.

Matthew 6.26-28

7. Foraging

Such an imaginative child
that one
reading, immersing herself
in another world

A thoughtful teenager
she is
wandering about, foraging
in nature

A contemplative young woman
is Bodhi
seeking, connecting her heart
in deeper meanings

Reflection: Way

We're finding our way, as we journey.

For most of my life, I deeply held that our spiritual journey is primarily about believing particular things and behaving in certain ways. I've been discovering, more recently, how life is about learning to love - freely, abundantly and expansively.

Jesus referred to himself as 'the way' (John 14.6) and emphasised that the most important priorities in life are loving God, loving one's self and loving others (Matthew 22.37-39). Deepak Chopra says, 'Love is the beginning of the journey, its end and the journey itself.'

The way is love.

How are you becoming more compassionate with yourself and with others?

What does loving freely and abundantly look like for you?

In what ways is your spiritual journey expanding your love?

Is something shifting in your relationship with God?

How is love shaping your life priorities?

As a practice today, you could write to someone, sharing your love and appreciation for them. Alternately, you could be vulnerable and ask a trusted friend how they see that you're becoming more loving.

8. Momentary Pause

Dawn air slightly chill
imperceptibly fragrant.
I breathe in through my nostrils
and my chest expands.
Pause.

Exhaling from my mouth
as my lungs squeeze.
Breath warm and moist
a mist that disappears.
Another pause.

Seeing the sunrise.
Watching the trees.
Meditating.
Commuting.
My love is speaking.
This meeting.
Thanks for our meal.
My child smiles.
Walk in the evening.
Night time examen.
Pause.

9. Unitive

I've been discovering
God is unitive.
They're bringing all things together.

No, God isn't punitive
and he isn't angry or untethered.

I'm uncovering
how God is so creative.
She keeps making her creation.

And God is regenerative
drawing us into their restoration.

10. Contemplative

Quietly we listen
to the whispering wind
gaze
at the wind-swept ocean
concentrate
on the vast horizon

11. Fields

I awake in a field
with deep, deep contours
richest soil
flowing streams
abounding with life

Together we cultivate these fields
with love

12. Deeply Shaped

I came to you
when your heart was broken
when Melanie had gone

I grew in you
where you felt such deep pain
where she had also been

You comforted me
when the grief enfolded you
when you couldn't hold her

How deeply the loss
of this dearly loved little girl
has shaped our soul

For my mum, Gail. My 2 year old sister Melanie died in April 1971.
I was born in November 1972.

13. Unseen

Go to your inner room
the place that's unseen
the place in your heart
where only God sees

Matthew 6.6

14. Worship

Ambling a busy street
attentive to the faces of passers-by.

Standing still in the forest
lost in the experience of these trees.

Sitting on the fragrant ground
aware of my dog's loving devotion.

Lying foetal position
quietly contemplating my beloved.

Being in this moment
and cherishing ...

Justin Simpson

everything that is God.

Reflection: Movement

The journey requires movement.

In the COVID lockdown of August and September 2020 in my home state, I walked over 500km (within 5km of my home). During that time, I also moved spiritually, as my belief system and my ego were deconstructed, and I reconnected with God.

Our movement can be gentle or strenuous. It can involve physical activity. It can be movement of the soul: inward with reflection; downward with grief or loss of ego; upward, drawn into transcendence; and outward with a sense of immanence and purposeful action.

These soul movements can be energising and feel positive, or difficult and disorienting. Sometimes they are quite dramatic. Other times they are barely discernible and their significance is only recognised in hindsight.

From where have you travelled?

How are you moving now?

Do you feel any pain or obstacles as you move?

What can you see up ahead?

As a practice with this reflection, perhaps you'd like to take a long walk, or try swimming, yoga, dancing or walking a labyrinth.

15. Just the One

Are you hurrying
worrying
scurrying
feeling distracted
exhausted
by all you have to do?

Relentless self
expectations
constant demands
for action
there are
just
too
many
things.

Have you been yearning,
learning,
leaning in?
Seeking to be still
and refilled
in what you're becoming?

Let's sit quietly
together.
Share our heart
with each other.

Few things
really matter,
perhaps
just the one.

Luke 10.38-42

16. Greening

Under a manna gum
two hundred years old
healthy and growing
the man paused.

Above the unseen roots
deep in the ground,
nourishing, strengthening
he loved what he'd found.

He looked up
to the canopy
reaching upward and outward
breathing, synthesising.

With thousands of gumnuts
all over the tree
budding and seeding
the man felt free.

17. Inside Love

When we love
  we live within God
    in Mystery
      inside Love's
        spacious interiority.

        In our love
          God dwells in us
            Love is within.
              Being Itself through
              our inmost being.

            As we love
              in Love, with God
                we're entwined
                  deeply intermingled into
                the Divine.

1 John 4.16

18. Pneuma

Gentle wind
across my face
dancing among the trees

a deep river
within your soul
meandering through the land

the energy
in every living thing
animating our world

God is Spirit

John 4.24

19. No Separation

Separation, as mystics and awakened beings have seen, is an illusion. One mystic proclaimed, God and I are one. And love your neighbour as your self. Another wrote, together we are one, like a human body. Also, nothing separates us from God's love. There is no separation, you see. Every being, everything, we are all one.

20. Quietly Growing

They scattered seed on the ground.
Night and day, whether they are asleep or awakened
the seed sprouts and it grows
though they don't really know how.

All by itself, grain grows from the soil
first the stalk
then the head
and finally the kernel.

Imagine Divine movement.

Mark 4.26-29

21. Skimming Stones

Djerrang
flowing, changing constantly
forming all it streams over.

The stone
smoothed and equally weighted
shaped over millennia.

A child skims a stone on the river.

The spinning stone
bounces over the surface
again and again.

Then, losing momentum
it sinks down
into the river.

Djerrang is a river in northern Victoria, also called the Ovens.

Reflection: Sojourners

We need travelling companions.

I've enjoyed the friendship of Quaker friends as I've journeyed. They've supported and encouraged me as my faith is being reshaped.

You are not alone in your journey. Perhaps it's your sense of God, human friends, your ancestors, a pet, a writer, podcaster or faith community. Even these poems can be companions for your journey.

Sometimes we need to find new travelling friends. This can be because our discoveries about life and God don't fit the paradigm of our family or faith community. We need a few trusted sojourners with whom we can move and learn. They may be quite different from us in age, ethnicity, culture, social perspective or religious background.

With whom do you currently share your life journey?

Is there someone you'd like to invite into what you're experiencing on your travels?

Is someone coming towards you, seeking your companionship in their spiritual journey?

As a practice, you could invite them for a quiet walk, or to sit in nature or read these poems together.

22. Awakening

Painful aching
a deep-felt breaking
then maybe an awakening

A profound awareness
sense of presence
this spaciousness
and then perhaps our oneness

23. Very Being

Your Love
your Life
your Light
becomes ours

Your Presence
is with us

Your Being
is our very being

24. Heartbeat

Your beloved leans back
resting against you
listening to your heart

and here
your inner life
your divine connection
your love
can become ours

John 13.23-25

25. Confluence

Into each other, ancient creeks stream
a meeting place
of waterways and people

Our hearts can flow together
a sacred space
of consciousness and love

Near my home, the Dandenong Creek and Bungalook Creek confluence.
This joining of these waterways was a meeting place for the Wurundjeri people.

26. Lovingkindness

May we awaken
commune
and
move with Being

May we be
full of love
and
free from suffering

27. Animated

Just now as I am sitting
   three magpies have landed right nearby
gurgling and warbling
   their faces to the sky.

A gentle breeze is blowing
   moving flowers and the trees
the morning sun radiating
   on the insects and the bees.

They are all so animated
   the world has come alive
everything feels connected
   with me and these magpies.

28. In the River

I constructed a small dam
putting all myself into it
placing rock upon rock
trying to wall up the river

Floodwaters swelled
demolishing my little structure

Afterward I bent down
and began shifting what remained

Into the deeper water I wade
lie backward, arms outstretched
and moving with its flow ...

Justin Simpson

I let myself go in the river

Reflection: Rest

We need to rest and replenish to keep going.

A lovely aspect of my recent journey has been connecting with and being in nature. Sitting quietly outdoors, resting my hand on a tree, watching the birds, smelling the wind, feeling the earth with my feet.

We need little rests on this journey. Rest for our bodies, minds and spirits. We need to experience how we're part of the much larger whole. Space to pause and reflect. Time to integrate our lives and let the paradoxes of our journey come together.

As Winnie the Pooh suggested, 'Let's start by taking a smallish nap or two.'

As a practice today, perhaps you could spend half an hour sitting under a tree, or a day near a stream or ocean, or an evening under the stars. Maybe you could just write in your journal or doodle in your notebook. You may even go to bed early.

As you rest, what are you noticing around you?

How are your physical and emotional energy levels?

How are you sleeping?

What restorative activities do you need to replenish and sustain you for the next part of your journey?

29. The Cliffs

Millenia
of continual waves
gradually eroded
solid rock.

Crashing storms
opened
the cracks

Decades
of earnest seeking
slowly shaped
my soul's contours

Now letting go
reveals
my true heart

30. Participation

'That's so divine!' she'd say:
the glowing sunset
beautiful food
a wonderful experience

She's sensing, participating in the Divine:
in everything
with everyone
within her too

2 Peter 1.4

31. It's Being

Connected and aware
breathing a wordless prayer
giving Mum's hand a gentle squeeze
wandering among the trees

Knowing beyond thinking
loving without clinging

Present, contemplative
like gazing at the waves
cradling a newborn
your arm around a loved one

Slowing and seeing
it's becoming and being

Justin Simpson

Reflection: Perspective

We see new things as we journey, and we see things differently.

While I walked around my surrounds during months of lockdown, I discovered local topography and plant life I hadn't noticed in 20 years. I even found a local manna gum tree, reported to be over 200 years old. And in those hours and hours of walking, my perspective of God, the world and myself gradually softened and changed.

When we move to different vantage points, we can see new things and develop a broader spiritual perspective.

What are you seeing at the moment?

How has your perspective - of yourself, God, your connection with the world - recently changed?

How are pain, uncertainty, ambiguity being integrated in your outlook?

Is there a spiritual practice that's helpfully reshaping your perspective?

As a practice today, you could go to a geographically high location that gives you a wide view. Or you could visit a cultural place you've not visited before. Write down or draw how you're seeing life, yourself, others or God in new ways.

Further Steps

Our journey can involve a spiralling path.

You may want to keep reading the poems each day, exploring their layers, and continuing to deepen your contemplative journey and perspective.

I would love to hear how you have engaged with these poems and reflections, and how you've grown in your journey with contemplation, creativity and community. Please feel free to email me personally via:
justin.joshua.simpson@gmail.com

Justin Simpson

Acknowledgements

My journey to *Journey Companions* has been shaped by many companions along the way. So many people have significantly influenced and helped form me spiritually, going back even to my childhood. I'm thankful for each person who's accompanied me at different stages in my life.

Special thanks to Deb, Liam, Alannah and Callum for your love, kindness and patience - and for challenging me to be my authentic self! Mum, Dad, the Menzies, Crothers and Parrys, thanks for your love, generosity and example. I'm glad to share life with you all.

Thanks Paul Rayside, Brett Mitchell and Trish Becker for deeply investing in me, my spiritual journey and leadership in formative years. My love and thanks to the SU family, who encouraged my leadership and nurtured my spiritual growth and evolution, particularly Chris Helm and Naomi Swindon.

Deep gratitude to my friends in our online Quaker group, for cultivating my contemplation and encouraging my poetry. It's beautiful to be in community with you.

Thanks to Myrtle and Alan Trubody for seeing *Journey Companions* as a book before I could. Michelle Peterie, many thanks for your encouraging and insightful spiritual and literary guidance in shaping these poems and this book.

Thanks to the Quaker Thanksgiving Fund Committee and NSW Regional Meeting for helping resource this publication.

My appreciation to David Tensen for guiding me when I was at 'the wall', encouraging me to explore both contemplation and poetry on my journey outwards. Thanks too for helping me bring *Journey Companions* into the world.

Love Evolves

Our love grows
emerges and evolves
as the Circle flows
converges and revolves

Finally, my deepest thanks to the Circle of Life - God, Spirit, Christ - who keeps bringing me, bringing us, into ever-deepening love. A wonderful journey companion.

Journey Companions

CPSIA information can be obtained
at www.ICGtesting.com
Printed in the USA
BVHW010006020223
657634BV00018B/290